A CHILDREN'S BOOK ABOUT FINDING YOUR OWN FLAWS, THE ART OF DOUBLE-CHECKING, AND NOT MAKING ASSUMPTIONS

HOW TO NEVER BE WRONG

WRITTEN BY
CHARLOTTE DANE

COPYRIGHT (C) 2023
CHARLOTTE DANE AND
BIG BARN PRESS

One beautiful day, Willow went on a treasure hunt in her backyard. She used a cool tool called a metal detector to help her find treasure.

Suddenly, the metal detector beeped really loudly!
Willow was so excited to see what she found.
It was a beautiful pendant with a shiny blue gem in the middle!

Willow got really happy when she thought about where the pendant came from. Maybe it belonged to a brave pirate or a magical fairy princess! What if a nice dragon accidentally dropped it from the sky? Or maybe an alien owned it and left it behind as a hint to find his spaceship. And maybe, just maybe, it's just special pendant that gives you three wishes if you rub it!

She was bursting with excitement to tell her teacher and friends about her amazing discovery and her ideas about where it came from.

But when Willow showed her treasure to her teacher and classmates, they were impressed but had different ideas. They thought it might belong to someone in Willow's family or a bird dropped it on the place years ago.

Willow felt upset that no one believed her theory! She was so angry that she stomped her feet and stormed out of the classroom. While she was leaving, the pendant fell out of her bag.

Luckily, Willow's friend Winston cleaned the room that day and found the pendant. But when he wanted to give it back to Willow, she said she didn't want it because she had given up on her theory after what had happened.

Winston encouraged and explained to Willow that it's important to listen to other people's ideas because it helps make our own ideas even better. Sometimes, we need to pay attention to things that don't match our ideas because we can learn so much from them!

"Willow, let me tell you something. This is super important and you must remember these three things. First, If someone doesn't agree with your theory, don't get angry with them."

"Instead, be curious about why they didn't agree. Seek to find truth, not prove that you are right."

"One time, I had a theory that I could fly if I flapped my arms really fast like a bird. I was so sure it would work! But then, two of my friends thought didn't agree that doing that can make me fly."

"Instead of getting angry and proving I'm right, I took a moment to think and wonder why they thought differently. I also felt relieved! If what they're saying is true, then it's good thing I didn't jump off the roof and flap my arms."

"When I asked about their idea, one of my friends explained that we are much heavier than birds, while the other one said that I'll just get tired if I flap my arms too fast. As I listened to them, I took note of each information because I want to study them for later."

"You see, when we are curious, we can learn what's wrong with our theories and be a little closer to finding out what really works."

"Next, after writing down the ideas that didn't agree with your theory, try to address each point with your own ideas."

"This will help you find a way in your thinking and make sure you understand things correctly."

"That day, when I went home, I opened my notes and read the ideas my friends had about why humans can't fly"

"When I thought about what my friend said about humans being too heavy, I completely disagree because I've seen people fly with things like jetpacks or hang gliders."

"Lastly, if you can't find a way to deal with the information that doesn't agree with your theory, it might be because you're wrong."

"The next day, I went up to my friend who said that humans are too heavy. I tried to understand her perspective so I asked her why she thought that way."

"When she explained that she birds actually have hollow bones...well... I realized that humans don't! And the last time I gave my friend a piggy back, he was sooooo heavy! I understood that she was correct in this point."

"When I understood her perspective, I realized that my theory of flapping my arms really also had a flaw - I based it on what I saw in the cartoons. And the thing is, what happened in cartoons didn't always happen in real life."

"It's good to listen to other people's ideas and think about them, and it's okay to accept that our theories have flaws because we can learn from them and find better ways to fix them."

After listening to Winston, Willow finally realized the importance of being open to different ideas that don't match yours and finding what could be wrong in your theories.

When Willow thought about the ideas that didn't agree with her theory about the pendant, she became curious about them and used them to search for truth. She began to address them using her own ideas and understand her teacher and classmates' perspectives.

As she did, she realized that her theory had a flaw - it's impossible for the necklace to be owned by a fairy, alien or a dragon because they aren't real. It's even more impossible for a pirate to own it because they were always on a ship. And it didn't grant her three wishes when she rubbed it. That only happens in cartoons!

As Willow passed their big family portrait in the living room, she recognized that the pendant that her grandmother was wearing was strangely similar with the one she found in the backyard. It had the shiny blue gemstone in the middle! When she showed it to her parents, she learned the truth that the real owner of the pendant was her grandmother.

IN THIS HUMOROUS BOOK, WILLOW AND WINSTON LEARN ONE OF CHARLES DARWIN'S MOST IMPORTANT LESSONS – ASSUME THAT YOU ARE NOT CORRECT!

THE "I THINK..." BOOK SERIES IS ABOUT EMPOWERING CHILDREN AND EQUIPPING THEM WITH THE SKILLS TO GO TO SCHOOL, MAKE FRIENDS, AND VENTURE INTO THE WORLD. FOR MORE, VISIT BIGBARNPRESS.COM